St. Patrick's Day Facts & Myths

Uncovering the Myths, Legends, Traditions, and Celebrations Worldwide

James Christopher

ISBN: 9798882149542

Table of Contents

Chapter 1: The Historical St. Patrick

St. Patrick was not Irish; he was born in Britain around the end of the 4th century.

At 16, Patrick was kidnapped by Irish raiders and spent six years as a slave in Ireland.

During his captivity, he worked as a shepherd.

After six years, St. Patrick escaped by fleeing to the coast and convincing sailors to take him back to Britain.

The shamrock became associated with St. Patrick because he supposedly used it to explain the Holy Trinity to the Irish.

St. Patrick's given name was Maewyn Succat; he adopted the name Patrick upon becoming a priest.

The first official state-sponsored St. Patrick's Day parade in Ireland was not held until 1903 in Waterford. Before then, St. Patrick's Day was more of a religious occasion than a national celebration.

St. Patrick spent 40 days fasting on the top of a mountain, now called Croagh Patrick in County Mayo, Ireland.

He founded more than 300 churches and baptized over 100,000 people in Ireland.

Two letters by St. Patrick survive today: "Confessio" (a spiritual autobiography) and "Letter to Coroticus" (a denunciation of British mistreatment of Irish Christians).

St. Patrick is said to have used the native Celtic language and culture to help convert the Irish to Christianity.

Despite being one of the most popular saints, St. Patrick was never formally canonized by a pope.

St. Patrick's Day was originally a Catholic feast day and was made an official feast day in the early 17th century.

The first recorded St. Patrick's Day celebration in history was in St. Augustine, Florida, in 1601.

St. Patrick is also the patron saint of Nigeria, which was evangelized primarily by Irish missionaries.

The first parade held to honor St. Patrick's Day took place not in Ireland but in New York City in 1762.

St. Patrick is believed to have died in Saul, where he built his first church.

The site of St. Patrick's grave is disputed, with Downpatrick in Northern Ireland being the most widely accepted location.

Before green became synonymous with St. Patrick, blue was originally the color associated with him.

St. Patrick's teaching methods incorporated traditional Irish symbols into Christian ceremonies to ease the transition to Christianity.

"St. Patrick's Breastplate": A prayer known as "St. Patrick's Breastplate" is attributed to him, a call for divine protection.

"Confessio": St. Patrick wrote an autobiography known as "Confessio," detailing his capture, conversion, and mission in Ireland.

St. Patrick is credited with bringing Christianity to Ireland in the 5th century.

St. Patrick is the patron saint of Ireland, engineers, and paralegals.

March 17th, the day of St. Patrick's death in 461 AD, is celebrated as St. Patrick's Day.

Chapter 2: Celebrations Around the World

New York City hosts the largest St. Patrick's Day parade in the world, with over 2 million spectators annually.

Chicago dyes its river green every St. Patrick's Day, a tradition that started in 1962.

In Montserrat, known as the "Emerald Isle of the Caribbean," St. Patrick's Day is a public holiday.

Dublin's St. Patrick's Day festival lasts several days, featuring parades, concerts, and educational events.

Sydney Opera House and the Empire State Building are among the global landmarks illuminated in green on St. Patrick's Day.

Boston held its first St. Patrick's Day parade in 1737, making it one of the oldest in the United States.

St. Patrick's Day is celebrated in more countries around the world than any other national festival.

In Japan, the city of Yokohama hosts a St. Patrick's Day parade, reflecting the holiday's international reach.

London's St. Patrick's Day festival includes a parade and a festival in Trafalgar Square, showcasing Irish music, song, and dance.

Canada's longest-running St. Patrick's Day parade occurs in Montreal, dating back to 1824.

In Argentina, Buenos Aires hosts a large St. Patrick's Day party in its downtown district.

The town of Hot Springs, Arkansas, boasts the shortest St. Patrick's Day parade route, just 98 feet.

Norfolk Island in the Pacific Ocean celebrates St. Patrick's Day as a public holiday, a tradition introduced by Irish settlers.

The space station has celebrated St. Patrick's Day, with astronauts wearing green and sharing greetings.

In Russia, Moscow's St. Patrick's Day parade has been officially celebrated since 1992.

Savannah, Georgia, dyes its historic fountains green for the holiday.

South Korea's St. Patrick's Day festival in Seoul features Irish dance, music, and a parade.

Ireland's government began a campaign in 1995 to use St. Patrick's Day to showcase Ireland and its culture.

The Caribbean island of Nevis has a unique historical connection to Alexander Hamilton, and celebrates St. Patrick's Day with a variety of events.

In Birmingham, UK, the St. Patrick's Day parade is considered the third largest in the world after Dublin and New York.

Chapter 3: Symbols and Traditions

The shamrock is the most recognizable symbol of St. Patrick's Day, representing the Holy Trinity.

Wearing green on St. Patrick's Day is said to make one invisible to leprechauns, who would pinch anyone they could see (not wearing green).

Corned beef and cabbage is a traditional St. Patrick's Day dish in the United States, not Ireland.

The leprechaun, a type of fairy in Irish folklore, is commonly associated with St. Patrick's Day.

The first St. Patrick's Day parade in Ireland was held in Waterford in 1903; Dublin's first parade wasn't until 1931.

"Drowning the Shamrock" is a tradition where a shamrock worn on the lapel is put into the last drink of the evening.

Irish music, featuring instruments like the fiddle, tin whistle, and bodhrán (Irish drum), is a staple of St. Patrick's Day celebrations.

The phrase "Erin go Bragh" means "Ireland forever" and is commonly heard on St. Patrick's Day.

The color green is now associated with Ireland due to its nickname "The Emerald Isle," its green landscape, and its national flag.

St. Patrick's Day was originally a religious occasion; up until the 1970s, Irish laws mandated pubs to be closed on March 17

The Celtic cross, combining a traditional Christian cross with a circle surrounding the intersection, symbolizes the fusion of pagan and Christian beliefs.

Guinness, a popular Irish stout, sees its sales double on St. Patrick's Day, with over 13 million pints consumed worldwide.

"Kiss me, I'm Irish" is a popular phrase on St. Patrick's Day, often seen on buttons and shirts.

The snake is a symbol often associated with St. Patrick, who is mythically credited with banishing snakes from Ireland.

Irish soda bread, made with baking soda instead of yeast, is a traditional food enjoyed on St. Patrick's Day.

The harp, another symbol of Ireland, represents the nation and its people on St. Patrick's Day and is also the emblem of Guinness.

Irish lace, known for its intricate patterns, is another traditional craft celebrated on St. Patrick's Day.

Potatoes, a staple of the Irish diet, are featured in many dishes served on St. Patrick's Day.

The Blarney Stone, though not directly related to St. Patrick, is visited by thousands in the month of March for its legend of bestowing eloquence.

The Irish flag, with its green, white, and orange colors, symbolizes peace and is prominently displayed on St. Patrick's Day.

Chapter 4: The Modern Celebration

Social media platforms often feature special St. Patrick's Day emojis, filters, and hashtags to celebrate the day.

Many businesses and brands turn their logos green for the day, engaging in the global celebration of Irish culture.

"The Wearing of the Green" is a popular Irish ballad dating back to the Irish Rebellion of 1798, symbolizing Irish nationalism and rebellion.

The practice of dyeing rivers and fountains green started in Chicago in 1962 when city pollution-control workers used dyes to trace illegal sewage discharges.

Virtual celebrations, including online parades and concerts, have become more popular, particularly in response to global events like the COVID-19 pandemic.

Many cities around the world host annual road races, pub crawls, and other events to celebrate St. Patrick's Day.

Educational programs and cultural exchanges are organized to teach people about Irish history, culture, and the contributions of Irish immigrants.

The sale of shamrocks and other green merchandise spikes significantly in the weeks leading up to St. Patrick's Day.

Craft breweries and bars often create special St. Patrick's Day brews, including green beers and Irish-themed cocktails.

Restaurants frequently offer special menus featuring Irish dishes and green-themed foods for St. Patrick's Day.

St. Patrick's Day parades often feature elaborate floats, bands, bagpipers, and dancers dressed in traditional Irish attire.

Many schools and offices allow or encourage people to wear green or dress in costume for St. Patrick's Day.

Face painting, especially with shamrocks and Irish flags, is a popular activity at St. Patrick's Day events.

Baking soda bread, making corned beef and cabbage, and preparing green-colored desserts are common home traditions on St. Patrick's Day.

St. Patrick's Day has become a day for people of all backgrounds to celebrate Irish culture and participate in festivities.

Environmental initiatives, such as planting trees or participating in green-themed cleanups, are sometimes organized to coincide with St. Patrick's Day.

Irish language classes and cultural workshops see increased interest around St. Patrick's Day.

Charity events, including fundraisers for Irish causes and local community services, are often held on or around St. Patrick's Day.

The global lighting of landmarks in green on St. Patrick's Day is part of Tourism Ireland's "Global Greening" initiative to celebrate Irish culture and attract visitors.

Flash mobs performing Irish dances have become a modern and viral way to celebrate St. Patrick's Day in public spaces.

Chapter 5: Unusual Facts and Myths

The shortest St. Patrick's Day parade in the world occurs annually in Dripsey, Cork, running just 100 yards between the village's two pubs.

It's a myth that St. Patrick used the shamrock to banish snakes from Ireland; the island nation never had snakes to begin with.

St. Patrick's Day falls during Lent, but restrictions on eating meat were lifted for the day, leading to the traditional consumption of corned beef and cabbage.

There's a legend that St. Patrick once spoke with ancient Irish ancestors by sleeping on their graves.

In traditional Irish folklore, wearing green was actually considered unlucky, contrary to modern celebrations.

A 2012 estimate suggested that about 1 in 10 Americans claim Irish ancestry, contributing to the widespread celebration of St. Patrick's Day in the USA.

"Greening" efforts for St. Patrick's Day have included iconic sites like the Great Wall of China and the Pyramids of Giza. Some historians believe the color blue, not green, was originally associated with St. Patrick.

Ireland's government used St. Patrick's Day in 1996 to begin the 'St. Patrick's Festival,' a national campaign aimed at using the holiday to showcase Irish culture and boost tourism, which has since grown into a multi-day event attracting millions.

In Irish mythology, leprechauns were cranky souls, responsible for mending the shoes of the other fairies.

The largest shamrock collection was recorded by Guinness World Records, with over 1,000 different shamrock items.

An Irish toast on St. Patrick's Day might include the phrase "Sláinte," which means "health" in Irish.

The Irish government only began a campaign to promote tourism on St. Patrick's Day in 1995.

Corned beef and cabbage, a St. Patrick's Day staple in America, is more of an Irish-American tradition than an Irish one.

The Claddagh ring, a traditional Irish symbol representing love (heart), loyalty (crown), and friendship (hands), is often exchanged and worn around St. Patrick's Day to celebrate Irish heritage and values.

A rare phenomenon called "green flash" can be observed at sunset or sunrise, adding a mystical element to the celebration for some.

The 'Leprechaun Museum' in Dublin, opened in 2010, offers visitors a whimsical look into Irish folklore and the mythical world of leprechauns, particularly popular around St. Patrick's Day for those exploring the nation's cultural heritage.

In 2010, the Sydney Opera House went green for St. Patrick's Day for the first time, marking the start of a global trend.

Some people wear orange on St. Patrick's Day to represent the Protestant minority in Ireland, highlighting the day's complex cultural significance.

St. Patrick's lore includes the belief that he could raise the dead. This is part of several legends that depict him as having miraculous powers, illustrating the blending of myth and history in his story.

Chapter 6: Enigmatic Creatures and Mythical Beings

The Morrigan:

The Morrigan, a powerful deity in Irish mythology, is often associated with war, fate, and sovereignty. She is depicted as a shape-shifter, capable of transforming into a crow or raven, and is known to foretell doom and influence the outcome of battles. Her presence in tales underscores the complex relationship between life, death, and destiny in Celtic belief systems.

The Fomorians:

The Fomorians, depicted as a malevolent race of giants and monsters, are archetypal villains in Irish mythology, often clashing with the Tuatha Dé Danann.

Their battles represent the primal forces of chaos and destruction, opposed to the order and civilization brought by the Tuatha Dé Danann. The Fomorians' defeat signifies the triumph of culture over barbarism, a theme resonant in many mythologies.

The Fir Bolg:
Before the arrival of the Tuatha Dé Danann, Ireland was inhabited by the Fir Bolg, described in myth as the island's rulers. They are often portrayed as more human and less divine than their successors, embodying the qualities of strength, resilience, and connection to the land. The Fir Bolg's eventual defeat and integration into Ireland's mythic history symbolize the layers of invasion and settlement that have shaped the island.

Manannán mac Lir:

Manannán mac Lir, the god of the sea, is a prominent figure in Irish mythology, known for his mastery over the waves, storms, and navigation. He is often depicted as a benevolent protector of Ireland, offering guidance and aid to heroes with his magical boat, cloak, and sword. Manannán's tales highlight the Irish people's deep connection to the sea, reflecting its importance in their culture and survival.

The Cat Sidhe (Fairy Cats):

The Cat Sidhe, or fairy cats, are mythical creatures resembling large, black cats with a white spot on their chest. Legend holds that they roam the Irish countryside, possessing mystical powers. On Samhain, it is said the Cat Sidhe could steal a person's soul, unless protected by a ritual.

The Dullahan:

The Dullahan is one of Ireland's most terrifying mythical creatures, often described as a headless rider on a black horse, carrying his own head under one arm. The head is said to have a hideous grin and the ability to see across the countryside, even in the darkest night. This harbinger of death wields a human spine as a whip and rides forth to claim the souls of those who are about to die. The Dullahan's approach is announced by the sound of hooves and the cracking of his whip. It's said that no lock can keep him out, and those who watch his ride are often struck blind in one eye or doused with a bucket of blood.

The Clurichaun:

Cousin to the leprechaun, the Clurichaun is known for his love of drinking and mischief.

Unlike the relatively benign leprechaun, Clurichauns are said to be surlier and more prone to causing chaos. They are known to guard wine cellars and are often blamed for drunkenness and disorderly conduct at night. Legends say that if treated well, a Clurichaun might protect your wine cellar, but if mistreated, they will wreak havoc on your home and spoil your wine. The Clurichaun is a testament to the Irish love of storytelling and humor, embodying both the joy and the perils of overindulgence.

The Puca:
A shape-shifter and trickster, the Puca is known to change into various animals, but its most common forms are a dark, sleek horse, a goat, or a rabbit. The Puca has the power of human speech and is known for giving cryptic prophecies to those it encounters.

While generally considered benign, the Puca enjoys creating confusion and fear, especially at night. It is said that on Samhain, the Puca spits on wild fruits, making them inedible. However, in some tales, the Puca is helpful to farmers by bringing good luck to their crops and animals, reflecting its capricious nature.

These tales and legends, from haunting spirits to mythical gods, weave a complex narrative of a land where history, mythology, and the supernatural collide. Irish folklore's enduring appeal lies in its ability to speak to universal themes through the lens of the mystical, offering insights into the human condition, the natural world, and the unseen forces that shape our lives.

Chapter 7: Mystical Objects and Artifacts

The Lia Fáil (Stone of Destiny):
At the heart of the Hill of Tara lies the Lia Fáil, an ancient stone believed to roar when touched by the rightful king of Ireland. Its mythological significance as a symbol of sovereignty and destiny underscores the deep connection between the Irish people, their land, and their leaders. The Lia Fáil epitomizes the intertwining of Ireland's mystical past with its historical reality.

The Sword of Light (Claíomh Solais):
The Sword of Light, a weapon of invincible power, appears in several Irish myths, most notably in the hands of heroes like Fionn mac Cumhaill. This magical sword could cut through any barrier and was said to be so bright that enemies were blinded by its light.

The sword symbolizes the triumph of light over darkness, truth over falsehood, and embodies the heroic qualities of bravery and righteousness.

The Four Treasures of the Tuatha Dé Danann:

The mythology of Ireland speaks of four magical treasures brought by the Tuatha Dé Danann: the Stone of Fal, the Spear of Lugh, the Sword of Light, and the Cauldron of Dagda. Each artifact possessed unique powers, symbolizing the elements of earth, air, fire, and water, and together, they represented the sovereignty and prosperity of Ireland. These treasures are central to Ireland's mythological heritage, embodying themes of power, protection, abundance, and balance.

The Shamrock:
While not a mystical artifact in the traditional sense, the shamrock holds a mythical place in Irish folklore as a symbol of the Christian Holy Trinity, attributed to St. Patrick. Its significance goes beyond religious symbolism, embodying the spirit of Ireland and its culture. The shamrock is a national symbol, representing identity, faith, and the interconnectedness of all things.

The Harp of Dagda:
The harp of Dagda, a god-like figure in Irish mythology, was said to control the seasons and even the passage of time. This magical instrument could summon joy or sorrow, peace or war, demonstrating the power of music to influence the world.

The harp, now a symbol of Ireland itself, signifies the deep cultural importance of music, storytelling, and the arts in Irish life, weaving together the threads of the past and present.

These chapters unveil the rich mosaic of Irish folklore, blending the magical with the mundane, the heroic with the humble. They offer a glimpse into a world where the land is alive with stories, and every stone, hill, or river has its own tale. Ireland's myths and legends continue to enchant, reminding us of the power of imagination to shape our understanding of the world and our place within it.

Chapter 8: Hauntings and Supernatural Occurrences

The Haunting of Leap Castle:
Leap Castle, considered one of the most haunted places in Ireland, is reputed to be home to a host of spirits, including a malevolent entity known as "The Elemental." Its bloody history of clan battles and hidden dungeons, where victims were thrown to their deaths, has left a spectral imprint on the castle. Ghostly apparitions, sudden drops in temperature, and the feeling of being watched are common experiences, reinforcing the castle's reputation as a nexus of paranormal activity.

The Ghosts of Kilmainham Gaol:
Kilmainham Gaol in Dublin, a former prison now a museum, is said to be haunted by the spirits of former inmates, including those of political prisoners executed for their roles in various uprisings. Visitors and staff report eerie sensations, unexplained sounds, and sightings of ghostly figures, suggesting the walls of Kilmainham still echo with the despair and resolve of its prisoners, making it a poignant site of supernatural interest.

The Lady of Malahide Castle:
Malahide Castle, with parts dating back to the 12th century, is said to be haunted by the ghost of Puck, a jester who fell in love with a lady above his station. After his murder, his spirit remained, bound by unrequited love and loyalty to the castle.

Sightings of Puck, along with other spectral figures believed to be former residents, add a layer of mystical intrigue to the castle's rich history.

The Ghost of Anne Roche at Roche Castle:

Roche Castle, with its storied past and architectural beauty, is rumored to be haunted by the ghost of Anne Roche, a woman who lived and tragically died there under mysterious circumstances. Visitors and locals have reported seeing her forlorn specter wandering the castle ruins at night, often described as wearing a white dress, symbolizing her eternal search for justice or peace.

The Spirits of Charles Fort:

Charles Fort, a star-shaped military fortress in Kinsale, is said to be haunted by the ghost of a bride who leaped to her death upon hearing falsely of her husband's demise in battle. Known as "The White Lady of Kinsale," her apparition is said to roam the fort, mourning her lost love. The fortress's history of siege and conflict has left an imprint of sorrow and unrest, with tales of other spirits, including soldiers and prisoners, also reported.

The Shelbourne Hotel Ghosts:

The Shelbourne Hotel in Dublin, a landmark of luxury and history, reportedly houses several ghosts, including a little girl named Mary Masters, who died of cholera in the 19th century.

Guests and staff have recounted experiences of eerie chills, unexplained noises, and sightings of apparitions, contributing to the hotel's mystique and allure as a place where the past intersects with the present.

The Haunting of Loftus Hall:
Loftus Hall, located on the Hook Peninsula, is often cited as Ireland's most haunted house. Legend has it that during a storm, a mysterious stranger who was revealed to be the devil visited the mansion. After his exposure, he vanished through the roof, leaving a dark presence in the house. Sightings of the dark figure, along with the ghost of a woman believed to be Lady Anne Tottenham, who was driven to madness by the encounter, have been reported, making Loftus Hall a focal point for paranormal investigations.

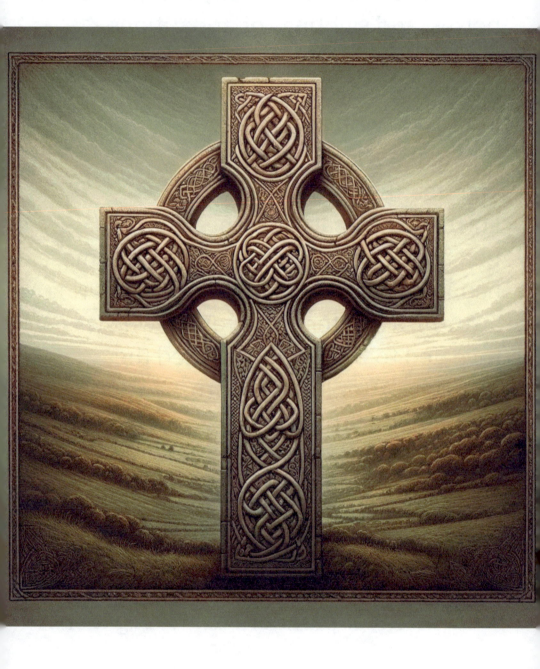

The Phantom Coach of Ballyheigue:
In Ballyheigue, tales are told of a ghostly coach drawn by headless horses and driven by a headless coachman, seen racing towards the cliffs where it vanishes into the night. This haunting spectacle is linked to a tragic accident where a coach plunged off the cliffs, leaving no survivors. The phantom coach is said to reenact this tragic journey, especially on dark, stormy nights.

These additional stories further illustrate the depth and variety of Ireland's hauntings and supernatural occurrences. Each tale is a thread in the larger tapestry of Irish folklore and history, blending the mystical with the tangible and continuing to fascinate both locals and visitors with an interest in the paranormal.

Chapter 9: Folk Tales and Legends

The Children of Lir:
One of Ireland's most poignant myths is the tale of the Children of Lir, who were turned into swans by their jealous stepmother. They spent centuries wandering the lakes and seas of Ireland, singing songs of such beauty that all who heard them were moved to tears. This story speaks to themes of loyalty, suffering, and the endurance of the spirit, reflecting deep cultural values around family and resilience.

The Salmon of Knowledge:
The legend of the Salmon of Knowledge is a foundational tale of wisdom and destiny in Irish mythology. It tells of a magical salmon that possessed all the world's knowledge.

Fionn mac Cumhaill gains this knowledge by accidentally tasting the salmon while cooking it for his mentor, imbuing him with wisdom and foresight. This tale underscores the value placed on knowledge and the sometimes unexpected paths to acquiring it.

The Legend of Knockmany:
The Legend of Knockmany involves Finn McCool and his wife, Oonagh, outwitting the giant Cucullin. Oonagh's cleverness saves Finn by disguising him as a baby, leading Cucullin to flee in fear of the "baby's" strength. This story, among many involving Finn McCool, celebrates wit over brute strength and highlights the importance of intelligence and cunning as valued traits.

The Legend of the Claddagh Ring:
The Claddagh ring, with its symbols of a heart held by two hands with a crown above, originates from the fishing village of Claddagh in Galway. The legend tells of a fisherman, Richard Joyce, who was captured by pirates and taught the craft of goldsmithing while in captivity. Upon his return to Claddagh, he created the ring as a token of loyalty, friendship, and love. This romantic tale is deeply embedded in Irish culture, symbolizing the country's values of love, friendship, and loyalty.

St. Brigid's Cloak:
The legend of St. Brigid's Cloak tells of how she spread her cloak over a large area of land to convince a local chieftain to donate it for the construction of a monastery.

As her cloak miraculously expanded to cover the desired acreage, the chieftain was amazed and granted her the land. This tale not only highlights the miraculous in the everyday but also celebrates St. Brigid's wisdom, faith, and the importance of community and sanctuary in Irish culture.

The Wooing of Étain:
This ancient Irish tale from the Mythological Cycle tells the story of Étain, a woman of unsurpassed beauty, and her love affair with Midir, a prince of the Tuatha Dé Danann. The story is fraught with transformation, enchantment, and rebirth, as Étain is turned into a pool of water, then a worm, and finally reborn as a human. The tale navigates through themes of love, loss, jealousy, and the cyclical nature of life, showcasing the complexity of relationships and the enduring spirit of love that transcends multiple lifetimes.

The Legend of the Bodach:
The Bodach, an Irish bogeyman figure, sneaks down the chimney to carry away naughty children. This tale served as a cautionary story, warning children against misbehavior with the threat of abduction by this shadowy figure. Beyond its disciplinary function, the legend reflects deeper societal anxieties about the safety and protection of children, embodying the universal fear of the unknown and the dark aspects of the world that lurk just out of sight.

The Twelve Wild Geese:
This folktale tells of a queen who, through a curse, turns her twelve sons into wild geese. The story follows the youngest daughter's quest to break the spell, facing trials of silence and sacrifice.

She must knit twelve shirts from nettles without speaking a word, enduring pain and misunderstanding to save her brothers. This narrative explores themes of resilience, the power of familial bonds, and the capacity for personal sacrifice for the greater good, highlighting the strength found in gentleness and the power of a determined spirit.

These tales, alongside others within the rich tapestry of Irish folklore, serve to educate, entertain, and impart moral lessons. They reflect the complexities of human nature and the profound connection between the Irish people and the mystical landscape they inhabit. Through stories of transformation, caution, and dedication, we gain insight into the values and beliefs that have shaped Irish culture and identity across centuries.

Chapter 10: Legendary Battles and Epic Feats

The Battle of Moytura:

The two Battles of Moytura are central to the mythological history of Ireland, depicting the conflicts between the Tuatha Dé Danann and the Fomorians, and later, the Milesians. These battles are rich in heroic deeds, magical interventions, and the struggle for the soul of Ireland. They symbolize the cyclical nature of conflict and the eternal fight between order and chaos, light and darkness.

The Cattle Raid of Cooley (Táin Bó Cúailnge):

The Táin Bó Cúailnge is one of the most famous epic tales of ancient Ireland, recounting the raid led by Queen Medb of Connacht to steal the prized bull Donn Cúailnge from Ulster.

The hero Cú Chulainn defends Ulster single-handedly, displaying feats of heroism, martial prowess, and the intervention of the gods. This tale explores themes of honor, pride, and the tragic consequences of conflict, echoing through Irish cultural consciousness.

The Feats of Cú Chulainn:
Cú Chulainn, the legendary hero of Ulster, is known for his superhuman feats, from the killing of the hound of Culann, earning him his name, to his single-handed defense of Ulster in the Táin (mentioned above). His training with the warrior woman Scáthach and his tragic death, tied to a standing stone so he could face his enemies even in death, embody the ideal of the hero in Irish mythology: brave, tragic, and larger than life.

The Exploits of Finn McCool:
Finn McCool (Fionn mac Cumhaill) is a central figure in the Fenian Cycle, known for his wisdom, leadership, and the exploits of the Fianna, his band of warriors. From catching the Salmon of Knowledge to creating the Giant's Causeway, Finn's adventures blend the boundaries between the human and the supernatural, emphasizing the power of knowledge, loyalty, and the enduring bond between the land and its people.

Oisín in Tír na nÓg:
Oisín, son of Finn McCool, is lured away to Tír na nÓg, the land of eternal youth, by a fairy woman. His adventures in this otherworldly realm and his eventual return to Ireland, where centuries have passed, explore themes of love, loss, and the bittersweet passage of time. Oisín's story is a poignant reminder of the transience of life and the timeless allure of the otherworld in Irish mythology.

The Second Battle of Magh Tuireadh: The Second Battle of Magh Tuireadh (Moytura) is a cornerstone of Irish mythological history, chronicling the epic confrontation between the Tuatha Dé Danann and the oppressive Fomorians.

This battle represents the struggle for Ireland's soul, pitting the cultured, skilled Tuatha Dé Danann against the brutish and tyrannical Fomorians. The victory of the Tuatha Dé Danann, led by the god Lugh of the Long Arm, marks the dawn of a prosperous era, signifying the triumph of light, knowledge, and culture over darkness and barbarism. Lugh's slaying of the Fomorian king, Balor of the Evil Eye, is a highlight, showcasing themes of prophecy, fate, and the cyclical nature of power

The Adventure of Connla:

Connla, the son of Conn of the Hundred Battles, is enticed by a beautiful maiden from the Otherworld, who offers him a life free from death and sorrow. Despite his father's pleas, Connla is drawn to the promise of eternal youth and joy, stepping into a magical boat that sails him away to the Otherworld. This tale explores the allure of the unknown and the tension between earthly duties and the desire for a transcendent existence. It reflects on themes of choice, the fleeting nature of life, and the eternal human quest for something beyond our mortal reach.

The Hosting of the Sidhe:
"The Hosting of the Sidhe" by W.B. Yeats, though a modern literary creation, is deeply rooted in the traditions of Irish folklore and captures the enduring spirit of ancient myths. The poem describes the fairy folk riding out on a moonlit night, capturing the imagination with their beauty and mystery. This piece speaks to the enchantment of the Irish landscape, haunted by the presence of the Sidhe, and reflects the continuous interplay between the visible and invisible worlds. It serves as a reminder of the thin veil between the everyday and the magical, urging us to look closer at the world around us.

These additional chapters on legendary battles and epic feats offer a glimpse into the rich fabric of Irish mythological and legendary narratives.

Through tales of battles for sovereignty, personal quests for meaning, and the poetic invocation of Ireland's mystical inhabitants, we are reminded of the enduring power of these stories to inspire, teach, and provoke reflection on the nature of existence and the pursuit of destiny.

Bonus: Spooky Irish Facts

The Banshee (Bean Sídhe):
The Banshee, whose name literally means "woman of the fairy mound," is one of the most renowned and feared figures in Irish folklore. She is a death omen, and her mournful wail is believed to foretell the death of a member of the family who hears it. The Banshee is often described as wearing a grey cloak over a green dress, with long, flowing hair that she brushes with a silver comb. It's said that the Banshee can appear in several forms, from a beautiful young woman to a frightful hag, depending on the lineage of the family she is haunting. Her cry is not seen as malevolent; rather, it is a lament for the impending loss, tying her closely to the Irish tradition of keening at funerals.

Leprechauns:

Leprechauns are perhaps the most internationally recognized fairies of Irish folklore, often depicted as small, elderly men dressed in a coat and hat who partake in mischief. They are known as cobblers to other fairies and are said to hide their pots of gold at the end of rainbows or in secret locations. According to legend, catching a Leprechaun grants the captor three wishes in exchange for their release. However, they are notoriously tricky to catch and even trickier to keep hold of, often disappearing when their captor's attention wavers

Changelings:

Changelings are fairy children left in the place of human babies stolen by the fairies.

In Irish folklore, this exchange is often attributed to the fairies' desire for a human child or to the wish to have the stolen child serve as a servant within the fairy realm. The changeling child is frequently described as sickly, unsatisfied, or exhibiting unusual behavior or abilities. The lore contains various methods to compel the fairies to return the human child, including treating the changeling harshly or outwitting the fairies in some manner.

The Dullahan:
The Dullahan is a headless rider, often seen driving a black coach pulled by headless horses. This fearsome figure is said to carry his own head under his arm; the head's eyes are constantly moving, and its mouth is locked in a deathly grin.

The Dullahan's appearance is an omen of death; he stops riding where a person is due to die and calls out their name, sealing their fate. Unlike the Banshee, his call is a direct harbinger of death to the specific individual he names. Folklore suggests that watching a Dullahan ride by might result in a basin of blood thrown in your face, or worse, being struck blind in one eye.

Merrows (Muirgheilt):
Merrows, the Irish mermaids and mermen, are said to inhabit the seas around Ireland. They are described as having green hair, webbed fingers, and a tail of a fish instead of legs. While Merrows are generally benign, stories tell of their interaction with humans, including romantic entanglements and marriages.

Their male counterparts are seldom seen and are said to be hideous in appearance, which might explain why Merrow women are often depicted as longing for human company.

Selkies:
Selkies are mythical beings capable of transforming from seals to humans by shedding their seal skins. According to folklore, if a human finds a Selkie's skin and hides it, the Selkie can be compelled to become a good but often pining spouse. If the Selkie retrieves its skin, it will return to its true form and the sea, leaving behind its human family. These tales often speak to themes of longing, loss, and the eternal bond between the sea and the land.

The Aos Sí:

The Aos Sí, or "people of the mounds," are the ancient spirits of nature and the predecessors of the Sidhe, living in the Otherworld but interacting with our world through the ancient burial mounds called "sidhe." They are respected and feared, with many traditions and festivals, like Samhain, rooted in the need to appease these powerful beings. The Aos Sí are considered guardians of the natural world, and offerings are still made to them in rural parts of Ireland.

The Dearg Due:

The Dearg Due, literally "Red Thirst," is a female vampire from Irish folklore. According to legend, she was a beautiful woman who was mistreated by her husband and died, only to rise from her grave to seek vengeance on men by seducing and then draining them of their blood.

The only way to pacify her spirit is by piling stones on her grave so that she cannot rise. This legend mixes elements of traditional vampire myths with Irish folklore, emphasizing themes of justice and revenge.

The Gancanagh:
The Gancanagh, known for his love of seduction, is one of the lesser-known members of the Aos Sí. This male fairy is notorious for enticing human women, often leading them to their doom. He is depicted as an irresistible figure, smoking a pipe and wearing a hat, and his touch is said to leave a mark that no human woman can resist. However, relationships with a Gancanagh always end in heartbreak for the human, as he will inevitably leave, causing the woman to pine for him until her death. This legend speaks to the dangerous allure of the forbidden and the consequences of desiring what we cannot have.

The Ghosts of Kilmainham Gaol: This historic prison in Dublin is reputed to be haunted by the ghosts of prisoners executed within its walls, including the leaders of the 1916 Easter Rising.

Charles Fort's White Lady: Charles Fort in Kinsale is haunted by the "White Lady," a bride who, according to legend, died on her wedding night and now wanders the fort mourning her groom.

The Hellfire Club: The ruins of this hunting lodge on Montpelier Hill are associated with stories of satanism, black magic, and a large black cat specter, believed to be the devil himself visiting the club.

The Ghost of St. Michan's Church: The mummified remains in the crypts of St. Michan's Church in Dublin are said to be guarded by a ghostly watchman who ensures they are not disturbed.

The Headless Horseman of Glenmore Castle: Legends tell of a headless horseman who roams the grounds of Glenmore Castle, carrying his head under his arm, searching for his lost love.

The Phantom of Loftus Hall: Loftus Hall is known for its haunting by a dark stranger, believed to be the devil, who visited the house in the 18th century and played cards with the Tottenham family, leaving a haunted legacy.

The Ghost of Anne Boleyn at Blickling Hall: Although located in England, Anne Boleyn's ghost is said to have Irish connections through her family. It's believed her spirit also haunts her ancestral home, Blickling Hall, on the anniversary of her execution, reflecting the tragic tales that link her to Ireland's history.

Deireadh an leabhair

Made in United States
Cleveland, OH
11 March 2025

15061624R00048